The Office Idiot Reviews

PETE SORTWELL

Copyright © 2013 Pete Sortwell

All rights reserved.

ISBN: 10:1490924329
ISBN-13: 13:978-1490924328

DEDICATION

For Mum and Dad.

ACKNOWLEDGEMENTS

I wouldn't be able to get my work into your hands if it wasn't for the help of the team I employ, they work extremely hard to make sure what ends up on your kindle is a high quality. These people are:

Julie Lewthwaite, for her continued sterling work on turning my ramblings into something that I can charge money for.
http://www.mlwritingservices.co.uk/

Graham D. Lock, for the excellent covers he's provided me.
http://www.peopleperhour.com/people/graham-d/animator-graphic-designer-and-illu/177926

I can't recommend these people enough.

INTRODUCTION

It's taken a little longer to get this book in your hands than I thought it would. I suppose writing something that was completely different from *The Village Idiot Reviews*, but also keeping the same style, was more of a challenge than expected. I've introduced pretty much 100% new characters, although there may be one or two that you recognise.

The first 'reviews' book has sold more than I ever thought it would. I hoped that maybe, one day, it would have paid for the cost of the editing and the cover art, however it has managed to fund this book and two more after it. It's sat in the top ten of parodies on Kindle store pretty much since release and has been jumping around in the overall humour charts, reaching number 13 at its peak. It has blown me away that people are buying it. Having said that, there was always going to be a series of these books. So, I'll stop bragging and introduce you to *The Office Idiot Reviews* ...

FOREWORD

Every office has many different characters. This one is no different. Apart from that, on top of being a group of different people, they're all idiots.

RONHILL MEN'S ADVANCED RACER SHORTS

Almost too short.

Norman Hogsbottom, the man, the boss, the supplier of plugs, is what the sign on my desk states. That's right, I sell plugs. However, being all of these things doesn't mean a man doesn't need to stay fit. I bought these running shorts after seeing the London marathon on TV. I found myself telling the office junior, Sandy, that I had already signed up and been accepted for next year's. I'm not sure what I was thinking; at the time I'd not run since I was at boarding school during shower time with Dirty McWandery hands, the games teacher.

These shorts seem to be what all the runners wear so I bought a pair. The date was set, I was going to go running one evening after everyone had gone home. I brought a honey sandwich from home for energy. I read that honey is good for that. Well, actually I read that bananas were good, but I don't really like them. I like honey though, so that was what was in the sandwich.

Once all my employees had left I changed into my shorts and navy singlet, wolfed down the honey sandwich, strapped on my Hi-Tec silver running shoes and headed out into the summer night.

I did fairly well, making it across the road and onto the tow path, only resting when walking down the stairway to it, then I headed off again. The lack of air poleaxed me about thirty seconds after that. Checking my watch I saw I'd been out the office for four minutes, which is embarrassing by anyone's standards. I decided it would be a good idea to walk and even ignored the taunts of 'Jimmy Savile' from the kids on the other side of the canal.

As I was walking, that's when it happened. All of a sudden I felt this stinging, burning pain on my pee-pee. It must have slipped out. The pain was worse than when I caught an STD in the navy. I thought I'd been shot for a second, then felt the wasp flying about in my shorts. Started thumping at my shorts trying to get the wasp out. This caused me some discomfort but it was the kind that gets worse over time, so when I was violently hitting myself in the groin area I wasn't feeling the physical pain of anything other than the wasp sting. The punching didn't seem to work so I went for the grabbing method; however, that did bring on instant tennis ball pain. The pain was starting to affect my balance, I was going light-headed in the way I have done before when I've fainted. Try as I might, I just couldn't get the wasp out. I began to panic. I could hear the kids laughing from the other side and I think I finally managed to get the wasp out before I slipped and toppled into the canal. That brought me to from the pain coma I seemed to have slipped into. Scrambling out, I'm sure I clambered over a dead sheep. It was the worst experience of my life.

I think it is partly to do with how short these shorts are and partly because I'm a messy eater when it comes to honey sandwiches.

My advice if you buy these shorts: if you're using them for running and not just sitting about the office (which is what I use them for now) then don't eat honey sandwiches in a messy fashion before you go out. The shorts are just too short. There is no way you can avoid any honey falling onto your pee-pee. Well, that's my experience, anyway.

Three stars as they are comfortable.

-Mr Hogsbottom

15 WHITE PAPER CARRIER BAGS PARTY BAGS

Great for carrying tall turds.

These are great. The handles are fantastic, as when you're carrying one containing tall items, such as baguettes, they can poke out of the corner and not touch any skin. Unfortunately I had to carry something far more sinister than bread-based snacks.

There's always a mess to clean up in the toilet. I know, toilets are *meant* to be dirty but the evil that lurks in the toilets where I work is like something out of a horror movie.

The other day I went in to attend to my cleaning duties and there was a log so big not even the business end of the steel brush would break it down. There was no way it was making it round the U-bend. It was stood up straight. I couldn't see any paper in the bowl either, so either it had been a clean break or it'd managed to stay prone during the flush. I soon discovered it was the latter as it wouldn't move when I flushed several times either. Seriously, it must have been painful for the person who put it there. Still, it being my job, I started the task of breaking it down with the toilet brush, although we already know how that worked out.

In the end I had to fish it out. It was the last resort, but after trying and failing to break it down with bleach there was nothing else I could think of. I'd been for lunch while the bleach took effect so had my newly vacant sandwich bag with me in order to contain the beast. I didn't have any gloves, so I used my trusty pliers to pick the gigantic turd up. The plan was to take it out the car park and sling it over the hedge.

As well as being huge, this thing also stunk to high heaven, too. It was dreadful and the faster I walked the more wind I generated, and the down force created forced the odour up my nostrils harder, although I didn't really equate the two things at the time, I just wanted it out of my office and out of my hands as quickly as possible. I think it was the bleach that finally made me faint. I'd forgotten I'd soaked it with the stuff. Thinking back, I know I should have sprayed it down with a flush or at least rinsed it under the tap; alas, I didn't and suffered the consequences. Those consequences mainly involving fainting on the back stairs then, when I woke up, rubbing my face with the hand that was still clutching King Kong's finger. It was the smell that woke me up. It was worse than any wake up call I've ever had. I thought I was in bed at home for a second. Although once I realised that I hadn't had a dirty bed accident the reality was even worse.

Now, I'm the cleaner, I knew I'd have to clean it up in the end — if it wasn't me, I'd have left it there for someone else to deal with, but I'd only have been summoned to deal with it once it was discovered. So, still feeling fairly light-headed, I picked myself up and carried on with my task. It was when I got outside that I realised the package had snapped. I'd had enough, though, and just got in the car and drove home after slinging the remaining half.

Unfortunately the offender has dropped the dirty bomb three more times since then, so I've ordered these. The handles make it easier to dispose of. I get a good bit of purchase behind my swing using them.

-John the cleaner

ADIOS MAX MAXIMUM STRENGTH WEIGHT LOSS TABLETS — 100 TABLETS

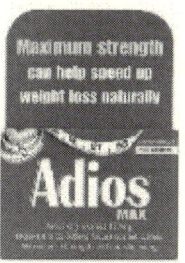

These won't make you sleep with the office ginger.

It is so dull in the office I work in. The boss, Mr Hogsbottom, is a posh boy who is as thick as a tin of soup. I have very little, other than ordering the boss's dinner and filling out a few forms, to do. I spend my time eating, it's nice to have a treat every now and then. Although, of course, this brings troubles of its own. I'm overweight. There, I said it. I'm a big fat bird.

I ordered these to try and help. I thought Amazon would be a better place to buy from as the ones I brought from a Chinese website did some strange things to me. I didn't want to eat at all, that was the good part, but I was sweating, erratic and wide awake all the time. My husband said they were like speed, although I've never taken drugs so don't know if that's true or not. All I know is those pills put me in a place I liked, to a point. The downside, other than the sweating, which as a fat person, I'm used to anyway, was that I liked everyone a lot more than I normally do. That and the increased libido. I was horny ALL the time. Which when you work in an office is no good, there is only so many times you can hide in the toilet trying to scratch that itch.

I'm ashamed to say, I ended up sleeping with Mark, the idiot health and safety officer. Well, we didn't even sleep, just met up behind the factory a few times. Every day. For a week. I think it was his breath repeating on me on the way home that made me realise something wasn't quiet right. I normally hate him. When I was on the Chinese pills though, I liked him immensely. I flushed the pills the Sunday after my week of passion with Mark and ordered these. I'm relieved to say that they've restored my sanity to normal and I was able to sneer at Mark with all my usual gusto when he tipped me the wink around half ten on the first day without my old diet pills. He got the message. It makes me shudder to think about now, though. There was a side effect to those other pills too. I had a hallucination. Just one. A giant fish outside the window, just swimming about. It was so real I didn't know I'd been seeing things until I sat down and thought about it. I mean huge goldfish don't fly about near second floor office windows, do they?

I've not seen as big a difference in the weight with these new pills yet. I'm hoping that they will kick in. My appetite has come back big time after my week of not really eating at all. I'm not expecting the weight loss I got from the other pills, but some would be nice.

The other positive thing about these pills is that I'm not finding myself dancing to any music. Least of all classical FM, which is what we're forced to listen to in the office. I was getting strange looks doing 'big fish, little fish' while Mozart was playing.

So, although I've seen little weight loss with these, I've seen other benefits. Not having had Mark's spicy sausage in my mouth for more than a week being the first one to come to mind.

Five stars!

-Margaret

VELCRO STICK ON SQUARES (PACK 24) 25MM BLACK

These help to never offend your favourite boy bands.

My name's Jeff. I like lots of things: I like Westlife, The Jackson Five, bananas, lots and lots of things. For my thirty-fifth birthday my mum brought me a Westlife T-shirt and a Jackson Five T-shirt. Great presents, but I have a problem. These are my two favourite bands of all time, ever. I can't choose between them! Never could. I generally have two Walkmans on me at a time, one playing Westlife and one playing The Jackson Five, using a specially made headset that I fashioned out of two sets and some tape that I borrowed from work. This method keeps them both happy and no one is left feeling left out in.

I decided to do the same with the T-shirts. I thought I could wear both at the same time; however, when I wore them under my shirt I sweated like I'd just been caught in the ladies toilet again. It was pretty hot and I couldn't manage it all day. I rapidly needed to think of a solution. Watching some YouTube videos of the bands one lunchtime, one in each window (again so no one felt left out) there was an advert where the head of the cartoon character kept changing to symbolise a different person. I thought that would be a good idea, it would also solve the two shirt sweating problems. I'd cut two heads off each T-shirt and mix them up, then I could wear both bands on the same T-shirt, under my work shirt, and I'd be supporting my two bands without smelling like a cheese sandwich.

I've done the cutting and it's worked fantastically well. These Velcro squares work really well for sticking the heads on the T-shirts. The best thing about doing it is that my mother thinks I've got a different T-shirt on every day and I can lie about how many baths I've had. All I need to do is change a couple of heads and I'm safe from getting wet.

I'd recommend these Velcro squares to anyone who is torn between two bands in such a way as I am. This stuff really works.

-Jeff

KENWOOD COMPACT JUG KETTLE, POLISHED METAL

Doesn't make your coffee taste like paracetamol.

I've taken to buying my own teabags and having this little kettle on my desk. I won't have anyone else make me a drink, either. I'm not sure if it's the water in this place or the lime scale in the kettle, but I kept feeling light-headed whenever I had a drink made from the kettle in kitchenette at work. Maybe the cleaners were not wiping the bleach off the surfaces properly. Whatever it was, I can't put myself through it anymore. I even found myself talking to the office weirdo after a cup and he kept on approaching me after that.

I don't need strange people in the office thinking I'm the go-to girl when they're bored. I want to get somewhere in this company, I don't put up with the mouth from the idiot MD for nothing. There's no way I'll be staying office junior for long. I'm quite happy to make my own tea to help make that happen.

-Sandy

GENTS' WOODEN PIPE

Let me smoke my pipe.

Mum refuses to let me smoke like one of my heroes, Simon Cowell. She says cigarettes are bad for you. I don't believe her though, the king of pop wouldn't do something that is bad for him. He looks after himself and his image. When I get enough money I'll be doing my teeth just like his, too, although I've read it costs thousands to get the natural square look that he has.

This pipe is a cracking buy, a really smooth smoke. I get cherry tobacco for it and really enjoy smoking it out the window of the toilets. I could go down to the smoking area, but no one knows I smoke and anyway, the smoking area is where I eat my bananas. They're all I carry in my lunch box and all I eat full stop, although I don't eat the bottom quarter of the banana. It's like a ritual, I think if I eat it something bad will happen so I stamp on it instead. It somehow seems cleansing.

The cleaner, John, asked me not to keep littering the smoking area and car park with bottom ends of bananas and he even reported me, but it's biodegradable so there's nothing he can do about it. I'm in the right.

The one thing about this pipe is that I think it could come with a case as it makes the inside of my pockets smell and on one occasion, when I hadn't knocked the smouldering ash out properly, catch fire. In my defence, someone was coming into the ladies and I had to hide it quick.

I might get one that looks more Sherlock Holmes style next time. Maybe if I looked more sophisticated then I could tell people I smoke.

-Jeff

MCCOY'S RIDGE CUT THAI SWEET CHICKEN FLAVOUR POTATO CRISPS 50 G (PACK OF 36)

I can get at least three bags in my mouth without choking.

Being the boss I get to do whatever I want and say pretty much anything I like, too. (Although I've got a list of words and phrases that could ultimately cost me money and damage my business's reputation taped to the jot pad on my desk. My lawyer gave me them after the last receptionist got funny about 'harassment'. So I'm careful now. I just sit in my plush, executive office all day giving the orders out in the morning and then dealing with any backlash from those orders.)

I normally dish them out via the office junior, Sandy, and let her deal with the normal staff who inevitably moan about what they've got to do on any particular day that doesn't involve sitting about gossiping and such like. I've got a lazy, dysfunctional staff team, but to be honest I like it that way as they'll always do whatever they are told, whether they moan about it or not.

I try to impress Sandy as much as possible when she's around. She's a nice girl and respects her boss, I think I get more respect out of her than any of the other workers.

They don't sell these crisps in the vending machine so having a box of them in my office is really something special. I've offered Sandy a packet before but she was too shy to accept. I've also shown my prowess by eating up to ten packets in front of her during our morning round up.

Sadly the showing off went badly wrong when I tried to impress her by shoving a whole packet in my mouth at the same time. I think I started choking because they're spicy. After I'd almost finished the first bag and was reaching for the next, I breathed in and the spicy dust got caught in my throat. I started to cough, which is not in itself impolite, but when you've got a pretty office junior in front of you and a mouth full of mostly soggy crisps it's disastrous. She didn't stay long after that, which was good because I was still struggling to breathe and if I'm honest I think I embarrassed myself a little bit.

-Mr Hogsbottom

SILVERLINE 868532 WHITE SAFETY HARD HAT

Sturdy, but attracts turd.

Part of being the office know-it-all involves telling people you can do things that you really can't, and that you've done things that you really haven't. In my role as health and safety executive it's good for people to think that I know what I'm doing and that I've done it before.

Of course, I'm not sure Mr Hogsbottom, the MD, really cares too much about health and safety. After a chair broke and he had to pay compensation for it, he brought me in to shout at in case it happens again.

This is the first buy of my new role and I feel wearing a hat like this lets everybody know who I am. I've made my own name badge, too, and I don't care what Mr Hogsbottom says, I'm not taking the word 'executive' off it and replacing it with 'officer'.

I wear the hat most of the day and I've managed to add one of the two clipboards that the company owns to my outfit, too. Strutting around checking everyone is doing what I've told them the previous day is something I was built to do. I developed the air of someone who is better than most in my last job as a correction officer. Although that didn't end well. They sacked me in the end for using undue force. Which is nonsense if you think about it. We were there to correct people and what better way to correct them than a good working over with the whacking stick, regardless of if they're collecting their dinner or causing a riot? Prisoners should be made of sterner stuff. If they can't take a punishment beating, then they've got little chance of lasting at being a criminal. Besides, sticks aren't issued for anything else. It's completely unfair that I got sacked for using an item for exactly what it was designed for. They wouldn't sack a chef for cooking up a lovely meal would they? No.

Anyway, I digress. Once the hat arrived I needed to test it to make sure it was robust enough to do its job and protect my lovely head, which incidentally was precisely what I was doing with the prison baton. Carefully placing the hat under the window on the stairs, I headed back up to the office and collected a few different items to drop on it from a great height.

The orange was destroyed by the hat on impact. It exploded, but left no marks whatsoever. So the next time Mr Hogsbottom doesn't like his lunch, it won't be me that suffers. The cleaners may have a bit more work to do, but my head won't swell up like it did last time.

The ceiling tile was also destroyed. There was a slight chip, but nothing to be concerned about. Hat: 2, Random Objects: 0.

Finally I dropped a brick. This hit pretty hard and bounced off, I've got to mark this as a positive. The hat didn't have any significant damage at all.

What upset me was, when I left the window and went downstairs to check the results of the brick drop, someone seemed to have moved the hat and a huge turd was in it. Not just a huge turd, but an old one that had started to turn white. At first I thought a bit of lining had come out, it was only when I felt the texture of it and then smelt my hand I realised what a sinister turn my experiment had taken. Someone had literally shat in my hat.

I couldn't wear it again after that. I've had to spend my own money on a replacement. I bought the same one, though, as it passed the 'drop' test, although I now keep the hat on my head at all times, without exception. I won't let anyone take it anywhere. I've not found out who hates me enough to save a turd for ages then wait until I'm away from my hat and dash out and lay the vintage turd inside. It's something that I'll be keeping a close eye on; if they're prepared to do that, just think what else they're prepared to do. It doesn't bear thinking about.

-Mark

AIR SWIMMER CLOWN FISH

Good at flying, bad at fighting broomsticks.

I often get bored at lunchtime so this gift from Mr Hogsbottom was much appreciated. He thinks I don't know he fancies my mum. She'd never go out with him, though, he's married anyway. It was nice of him to give me a job, though, and even nicer to give me this flying fish. I kept it at work, I didn't show my mother because that's what Mr Hogsbottom really wanted, I could just tell. I'm OK with the fact he bought it just to show off, but I got to benefit from it by playing with it.

I used it every lunchtime for a week. It's amazing how high it will go and not lose radio signal. Although I wasn't amazed for long. I got it up as high as the office window and someone started poked my fish with the window-closing stick. It was an epic battle, me and my fish stood our ground and even went in for the odd attack. If I'd had a flying shark we would have won as I could have chewed the stick. I didn't, though, and Terry the flying goldfish got caught on the stick and was flung around like he was a manky old teddy in a dog's mouth. I furiously tried to get Terry free, but his little flapping tail didn't have enough strength to fight off whatever evil was waving the big stick. The wild swinging of the stick caused Terry to become even more tangled as the air I had so lovingly blown into him left his body, then with one final lunge towards the sky poor old Terry was launched up and over the guttering to his final resting place on the roof.

I can't pretend I'm not upset. I enjoyed the summer lunchtimes flying Terry about in the car park. I'll find out who bashed him down with the stick. Then they'll pay. People in this office are going to wish they never upset me one of these days.

-Jeff

WAYFARER STYLE CLEAR GLASSES BLACK FRAMES RETRO LOOK

Almost as good as science goggles.

What with trying to dodge the advances of Donald, the office weirdo, I don't mind the annoyance of the MD. He's not weird like Donald though. Just annoying with the ability to ruin anyone's day.

For some reason, I think he tries to impress me by doing stupid things. The other day he was shoving loads and loads of crisps in his mouth and still talking. Of course he ended up choking, there was no other outcome. What I didn't like was that I was across the desk from him doing my usual task of humouring him with his latest strategic plan and I got bits of mangled up, soggy crisp in my face, hair and eyes. It was gross. I've brought these glasses to at least stop the chewed up mess going in my eyes, should he attempt a new record of seeing how many McCoy's chilli crisps he can get in his big fat gob.

-Sandy

SLEEP AID 25MG (DOXYLAMINE SUCCINATE) 192 TABLETS

Not as good as the Chinese ones.

I struggle to sleep at night sometimes. I just lie there with my head going round and round. I don't understand why my life is so terrible. Other people's lives seem to be great. Well, the people in my office anyway, I don't really know anyone else. They all have friends and social lives, boyfriends or girl friends. Me? I just have Sandy, the office junior to look at. Nothing else. My flat is tiny (as is my penis). Even the Russian girl that promised to come over and marry me got run over on the way to the train station. Apparently her handbag got flung so far it ended up in the river due to impact when the Fiat hit her so I couldn't even get my five hundred quid back that I'd sent her for the train fare.

It's all left me a very lonely person. These pills don't work too well for actually sleeping; although, they do make me feel better when I'm awake. I thought the only ones that could do that were the ones the doctor banned me from having for repeatedly phoning up for my monthly prescriptions every three or four days. There is only so many times you can tell them you lost them or that you're going on holiday. These ones do very much the same thing, though. I pop a couple in my tea and they seem to work better, something to do with them all being dissolved, I should think. It's a much more relaxing drink than alcohol. I even have a couple in the afternoon at work sometimes, just to loosen things up a bit.

Great product, I hope they don't get banned like the last ones I brought from the internet! They're my medicine.

-Donald

INFLATABLE MONKEY

A good present for a simpleton.

It's hard to think of what to buy the office simpleton when he doesn't open up much. All Jeff does is walk around taking messages from one desk to the other, ordering people's lunch and wearing his ridiculous T-shirts. However, it's an office so we have to celebrate everyone's birthday with false best wishes and cards that I have to buy.

The collection raised just under ten pounds, which is pretty poor even for this office. The huge Jackson Five card I ordered cost £7.50 of that so there was very little for a present. Jeff doesn't talk about much, not on a personal level, anyway. He seems to chant to himself a lot, but when talking to other people he just keeps the conversation to his favourite bands, bananas, and asking them to check their clothing label is not sticking out. Oh, and asking what message needs to go where. We have email in the office and Jeff isn't very good at delivering messages, so I'm fairly sure he is only kept on because Mr Hogsbottom pops round to see his mum on Monday lunchtimes. It's like a south of England version of Forrest Gump. But with a worse hair style.

I've heard Jeff talking about his pet, Peter, who he pretends is a monkey. I'm not sure what it actually is, but ascertained from his conversation that he liked monkeys. So that, coupled with the fact I only had £2.50 left and little to no motivation to leave the office to go in search of something in the pound shop, I found this monkey. I haven't blown it up yet but I'm sure it'll be fine. The point is it vaguely relates to something that he likes and it was cheap.

I'd recommend it for anyone looking for a present for someone they don't really care about, or a child. I'm sure a child would like it too, although a word of caution on that when I opened the box I could smell solvent pretty strongly and that was through the wrapper. Jeff will be OK though, he's a fully grown man — in body.

Five stars for me not having to leave my desk to get it.

-Margaret

APPLE IPOD NANO 4GB SILVER

Just needs two headphone sockets.

For so long I've had to carry two huge CD Walkmans about with me. I can never decide which of my favourite two bands to listen to, so I simply listen to them both at the same time. It saves the inner conflict. Using the CD players also required big pockets and although there's plenty of room in my trousers to house huge pockets, a CD Walkman does have the tendency to fall out when I'm running round the office delivering my messages to people in all the different departments. They're desks really, the company isn't that big, but Mr Hogsbottom, the MD, insists we call them departments because it sounds better.

I'm aware of the internet and the digital age, of course I am. I just don't know how to use it very well. However, when Mr Hogsbottom gave me a couple of these preloaded with every Jackson Five and every Westlife album ever released, including the live ones, I didn't need to know how to set them up, sync them or anything else, I was set! They're great.

The ear buds that came with these were really small, too. I've never worn this sort of headphone before, preferring to fashion one unit out of two over head- sets and use that to pipe two different songs into two different ears. I had to stick these ones right in, really tightly. It was when I ran up the stairs on my way into work on the first day of having them that I caught the long dangly wire on the banister. (I never take the lift, I worry that if it got stuck the battery would run out on my music and that it'd get hot and I wouldn't be able to keep my bananas at the optimum temperature to consume, and who likes warm bananas?) As I jogged past, not wishing to wait to get my bananas in the fridge, I was wrenched backwards. At first it was just a snag. I thought it was stuck on the bottom of my cagoule like both wires had been doing all the way into work so I just jerked my knee up to release it and carried on.

Sore ear.

The bud was in my ear so tightly that the wire snapped before the bud could fall out. It was a nightmare getting the broken ear bud out. The nurse at the hospital said I should never put any glue in my ear, even wood glue, and that ear buds were designed to stay put without anything keeping them there. She was kind enough to remove the other one, too.

I've since tested what the nurse had to say and she's right: iPod ear buds stay in your ear without the aid of glue. Who knew? It cost me the price of two new pairs, but they were cheap enough and if I ever get fed up of them I've got my trusty old homemade pair of over the top ones to fall back on.

These iPods are so cool, I can wear the tightest of tight trousers and still get them in the pockets without fear of them falling out. It's great. I've even seen these arm bands you can get for them. I'm definitely going to ask Mr Hogsbottom to get me them for Christmas. Although in the picture I saw of those the guy running was wearing tights and he had shorts over the top of them. I'm not sure what look he was going for. The eighties are over. The only thing left from that time is The Jackson Five and thanks to my iPods I can now listen to whatever song I want, wherever I want, without having to faff about changing a CD over and trying not to drop and scratch the disc.

I've a suggestion for Apple, if they're reading this: with all the technology they have nowadays, do you think you could invent an iPod that plays two different things at the same time with a couple of sets of headphone jacks on it? That would be absolutely ideal for my needs.

I'd also suggest putting a label on about using glue to keep the ear buds in, too, a word of warning at the very least.

I shall monitor this review for a response from Apple on my questions. Failing that I'll send them a letter outlining my ideas. They might even give me a job designing it. I can't imagine anyone has thought of something so brilliant before.

-Jeff

RED BULL ENERGY DRINK ORIGINAL 250ML REF RB0375 [PACK 24]

Doesn't make you dance to the news.

Sleeping had never been a problem for me when I started at this company twenty years ago; in that time I've had not one promotion. I've never even had a pay raise that wasn't mandatory with inflation.

Singled out is how I feel. Singled out, bullied and over worked. Even when I decided to work to rule, nineteen and a half years ago, it was the same: no one respects me.

I think it's the stress that makes me feel as bad as I do. I worry a lot, too. It only has to be a message from Jeff or an email asking that I attend a meeting with Mr Hogsbottom and it sets me off. I can't do anything for days. I've even requested that they come and ask me on the day of the meeting so I don't have it on my mind, but I'm sure it just made them ask even earlier.

The 'washing machine head' starts at night, round and round, the same thoughts. The only way I know how to lower the anxiety is to think about the lovely office junior, Sandy. Then I'm up even longer frustrating myself to the point of soreness. That, along with the sleeping tablets I take to try and drop off (which kick in about 8.50 a.m.) all make for one very tired Donald.

I first started taking Pro-plus tablets, which work to a point, but because they are in tablet form, I tend to take too many and end up shaking like a dog trying to pass the house keys it's eaten. This Red Bull is much better as it is in liquid form and allows me to pace myself throughout the day. I drink one on the way to work, one as soon as I get there (to make the coffee taste better), then I sip four throughout the morning before another one at lunch, again with coffee, and another four in the afternoon. As you can see, I like this a lot, so buying in bulk and getting it delivered saves my money and my back as I don't have to lug them all the way back from the supermarket and then carry them into the office.

I'm happy with the Red Bull. It's much better than the Monster I was drinking to start with. Monster is double the size and I went too far on that. One week had been a particularly stressful week and I couldn't switch my head off. Sandy wasn't talking to me and that just made things worse. I'm not sure what was up with her, busy I think. The antidepressants were not working, even when I sniffed them. The only thing that made me feel a little like doing anything other than sitting with my head in my hands was drinking the Monster and taking more of my sleeping pills. My position was; that at least I wouldn't remember how bad I felt. I ran out of my sleeping pills and had to look for something else. I remembered that Margaret had some pills that she'd been using for slimming. I've had pills like that before, back in the day, so went looking for them. They weren't hard to find, just sitting there in her handbag waiting for someone to take them. Margaret was off somewhere else, like she'd been a lot around that time. I necked a few, and headed back to my own desk via Sandy's cubicle; however, she was busy looking the other way as I walked past.

I only heard about what happened the next day in an emergency meeting with Mr Hogsbottom.

Apparently, I'd turned my radio up extra loud during the news and started dancing. Not only that, I tried to get other people involved. Sandy, first. She'd humoured me for a minute, apparently, then went and hid in the toilet.

Jeff was next on the list of people I annoyed. He got upset because, apparently I took his headphones off him and tried to listen to whatever it is he has on them all day, every day. When he ran off he decided not to go round the cubicle like normal people would, he went as the crow flies. Through every string-covered chipboard wall, taking desks, phones and computers with him as he went.

I was wrestled to the floor by Margaret and her bad back then locked in the cleaning cupboard. Apparently I started shouting Sandy's name over and over and confirming that I was a straight male regardless of what the people at school had labelled me.

The list of charges didn't stop there. It went on and on and ended up with me being found in the car park with my trousers round my ankles, dancing, rave style, in silence.

Thankfully, I've not had the same experience with Red Bull and I can drink it at work. Although I'm on my final warning. If anything happens again I'll be gone, Mr Hogsbottom says.

I think Sandy's forgiven me. Jeff hasn't, though. He won't look at me now. Just stares at the floor when he comes over to take messages. I've tried to apologise, but he won't listen. He just seems to be chanting. It weirds me out to be honest. I think I might need to get a job with some normal people. This lot are mental.

-Donald

SWAROVSKI ELEMENTS CRYSTAL FOUR LEAF CLOVER PENDANT NECKLACE 19"-CN9034SG

Good enough for a lover AND a wife.

Apart from being a boss and general saviour to a lot of local people, I'm also a lover and a husband. Not loving enough to stay faithful, but I do keep it to just the one other woman. I've had Julie on the side for years now. To be honest if it wasn't for the situation she was in with her son, Jeff, I'd have left my wife and settled down with her years ago.

Jeff's different. That's all there is to it. It isn't specifically called anything. He isn't thick or slow, in fact he's a bit of a wiz in regards to some subjects, he just has his ways and he's set in them. So a man coming into the house wouldn't be something that he would tolerate. Julie has accepted that's how Jeff is and until she finds someone else who is willing to put up with him, she's stuck with him and that's that.

I brought a couple of these lovely pendants for the two lucky women in my life.

With a cheeky grin I presented one to my wife on Valentine's Day. She was overjoyed. She knows how lucky she is to have me and a four leaf clover is exactly the right symbol to show her friends just that. Well, except for best friend, Esmeralda, she's not keen on me. A few years ago she rumbled my game and has taken every opportunity since then to put me down.

THE OFFICE IDIOT REVIEWS

She collared me about seeing me with Julie and after I realised lying was futile I admitted everything to her. She wouldn't grass me up, though, she doesn't want to see her friend upset. Although I notice that hasn't stopped her upsetting her with her vile opinion on me and everything I do. Ever since then, though, it's just one of the things in life I have to put up with. I suppose it's jealously. If I looked like a gargoyle that had fell from the side of a very high church I'd probably tell my friends that their partners were scum of the earth, too.

Giving Julie the necklace was great. She's so grateful for a little attention. She was jumping up and down with excitement so much the couple in the room underneath us in Happy Hotels banged on their ceiling and asked us to keep it down! We later put in a performance that also made them bang on the ceiling, but we paid less attention to that one. Unfortunately after we'd finished I tripped on my hastily discarded trousers and did that thing were you hop, trying to stop yourself going fully over. This was the point where the couple from downstairs got really annoyed with the banging and by the time I'd flushed the toilet the guy was banging at the door telling us to keep the noise down or he'd do me some harm. Although I've edited what he said, I'm too polite to repeat it. I didn't answer the door, engaging with those types of people never does any good. I was upset though as it completely ruined the second go I had on Jeff's mum. It was like having a little kid in the house that you don't want to disturb, only it was a maniac that had threatened to shove something somewhere.

We went off in the Roller and got a McFlurry after that. What more could any woman ask for? An expensive-looking bit of jewellery, an hour with me in a hotel, and a dessert on the way home to her son.

I might get them both the earrings to match next year.

-Mr Hogsbottom

SILVERLINE WR20 200 MM ADJUSTABLE WRENCH

Does the trick.

I've been getting upset with the receptionist in my office. She is making my life a misery. These will help me get her back for what she's done. When the time comes I'll just stand and laugh, right at her too.

-Jeff

SONY LIVEVIEW TOUCH GENERATION 2 SMARTWATCH ANDROID SMARTPHONE ACCESSORY

Great in pub quizzes.

I know I shouldn't, but from time to time I tell a few porkies. Just about things I've done, places I've been. I don't harm anyone by doing it, it's the opposite; in fact, I think my habit of embellishing things a little tends to put either a smile or a look of amazement on a person's face. Also, it got me my job and being a health and safety inspector is pretty important. It saves lives. Mr Hogsbottom, my boss, says I'm a great example to all I meet. Especially the kids I have but don't see. Their mother was a bit of a stick-in-the-mud so I binned her. I suppose when you have a husband that shines as bright as I do then it can be hard for the partner to live in the shadows.

I bought this watch to make sure I won the latest of Mr Hogsbottom's hare-brained 'team building' ideas, a quiz. Don't get me wrong, I'm bright as hell. The only reason I needed to take out an insurance policy such as this was in case the worst came to the worst and Hogsbottom picked some *really* tough questions. Even if I got one or two questions wrong it would be a catastrophe. My colleagues wouldn't be able to cope with the disappointment. Not in me, but in themselves.

It worked fantastically well, every question that came up I was able to search on Wikipedia right under security's nose.

The down side of looking for answers covertly in a quiz it

that it is also linked to your phone. So if, like me, you haven't got ten or twelve birds lined up like you normally have, constantly looking at something that tells you absolutely no one is trying to contact you can be a bit soul destroying. It's OK, though, because I've got a date with a local page three model next week. She'll be ringing me all the time after I introduce her to my ding-a-ling-a-do-dah.

I'd give this watch five stars. If the manufacturers would like to send me a couple of free ones I'd have no problem showing them to my contacts in the secret service, they could do with something like this.

-Mark

WAHL 79400-800 COLOUR PRO CODED MAINS HAIR CLIPPER KIT

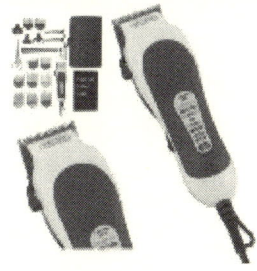

Need an artificial comb over? These are the kiddies for you!.

Losing your dad at such a young age is never a good thing to happen; well, unless he was Jimmy Savile and you were yet to hit puberty. I wasn't and neither was my father, so it pretty much sucked all round. The thing that is hardest for me now is that my memory of him has faded. I've filled my brain with thoughts of The Jackson Five, Westlife and bananas too much since then. I've got photos, though, and it's nice that I have. God knows what my brain would have turned the images I had into. I've always had a bit of an over-active mind. Not on learning stuff, more on creating things, stories and such like. Without the photos I'd have no doubt created some kind of afro, Jackson Five style, Irish Jesus figure.

Anyway, I'm getting off the point. I lost my dad and from all the stories my mother has told me about him, I want to be as much like him as possible. He loved The Jackson Five, that's where I got my love of them from, and if he was alive he'd love Westlife, too, I just know it.

From the pictures I've seen of him, he was a handsome man with an interesting haircut; bald on top with one side really long and then combed over the top. Now, not all of my hair falls out on its own, it doesn't even get pulled out when I'm in a rage anymore. In order to obtain the same hairstyle as my dad I needed to get serious and get it cut. I headed into the local barbers to get it done, but for some reason or another he wouldn't do it. Kept asking if my mum knew where I was and what I was doing. So I decided that I'd do it. What with YouTube videos on everything these days, I'd be able to get the look I was going for, no problem.

The cutting was fairly easy, although it took a few more times to get the line on the right side straight. Although I'm a master at it now and even shave the top of my head once a week with a normal razor to get the baldness just right.

This is my third set of clippers and seventh year of styling my hair like my dad. I think the look works for me and as my own hair falls out more and more (again not pulled as some people may suggest) the less I have to cut. If I couple it with a good dollop of Brylcreem, then it sits just right. It's a powerful haircut.

One day I'll be boss with this look. My dad was boss of everything he did, Mum told me. Apparently he used to get a job and be running the show so well that all the other employees would get jealous and make up silly stories about him to get him sacked. Dad didn't care, though, he'd just move on and get a different job and do well in that too. Well, until the people got jealous there, as well.

-Jeff

JACOB'S CREAM CRACKERS BISCUITS 300 G (PACK OF 12)

Too much cheese? Buy these!

Being the boss of a successful plug making company I don't have that much work to do, so much of my time is spend trawling the internet for things to spend my money on. I'm a bargain fan. This means that I sometimes end up with surplus items, food and such like. Normally I just drop it off down at the church food bank. I do this for a couple of reasons: a) to look great — I get the press down there and get a photo of me single handedly feeding the community, and b) to get rid of the stuff — seriously, I go too far sometimes.

I happened to find a glitch not so long ago that left me with more cheese than even I knew what to do with: £1 for 700 grams of the stuff. I'm not sure what I was thinking when I added 1000 items to my shopping cart. I didn't think for a second it would come. Unfortunately I was wrong, come it did, to the office.

It was a shame as normally I can hide the bits I get. Seventy kilos of cheese wasn't so easy to keep from the troops' beady eyes though. Like flies around dung, they were. 'Can I have some,' 'Can I take some for the children.' It was like Oliver all over again. Anyone would have thought I didn't pay them. I don't like to give the minions more than their pay. It creates an ethos of expectation. I don't pay overtime and I don't give time off for hours worked over. If they can't get their job done in the time I pay them for then there is a conversation that we need to have. However, on this occasion I did have the problem of too much cheese and after a week of supplying the food bank and eating cheese with everything myself, I still had far too much.

There was only one thing for it; I had to dish it out to my staff. In order to get the cheese eaten and not make out that it was a reward for anything, I needed to be inventive. What I did was; I got the guy who runs the food bank to come up, then asked him to stand next to me while I announced that we would be getting a load of cheese in, from them, as a thank you for all my charity work. I didn't discuss it with the chap from the food bank beforehand. During the announcement I had to assure him quietly that I wasn't taking back any of the cheese I'd given him, after he knew that he was OK with anything being said.

That's where these crackers come in. I chucked some good money after bad and got Margaret to cut a load of the cheese up and put it on crackers every lunchtime for a week. It didn't take this lot of gannets long to get through the lot. Margaret cut her hand doing it. I suppose that serves her right for being greedy. No wonder she has to take weight loss pills.

-Mr Hogsbottom

THE DICTIONARY OF CORPORATE BULLSHIT: AN A TO Z LEXICON OF EMPTY, ENRAGING, AND JUST PLAIN STUPID OFFICE TALK

It's like a dictionary to understand dickheads.

The shit my boss comes out with is like a foreign language. The other day I was sat there and realized I hadn't understood a single sentence he'd said in the whole five minutes he'd been explaining his new strategy. (A new strategy is something he has about once a week.) It went something like this:

'The details are still quiet fluid at the moment, however the real meat of the sandwich is firm, nailed down and in alignment with company policy. We're really bridging the gap here,' — he did the finger brackets here — 'we all need to embrace this move into a new phase of our development.'

If you have any idea what that means without reading this book then it isn't for you. I thought he was talking about someone vandalizing his lunch.

I've been here for a few years now and every week it's the same. Hogsbottom comes out his office and announces to the room that we all need to listen to what he's got to say, then he'll come out with stuff like this, go back in his office and nothing whatsoever will change. We don't even have a company policy. We barely have a company. If it wasn't for the fact that our products sell themselves and he holds a patent that means no one else can make or sell them, we'd be out of business in a week. I mean the world will always need bath plugs, won't they? There's no need for any of it. We just make plugs, keep on making them, then sell them. People come to us. Donald's job is to find new customers; I doubt he's done a day's work in the twenty years he's been here. The numbers never go down. I'm fairly sure it's some kind of phenomenon in industry that pretty much the same amount of product is made year on year and has been for thirty years. You'd think the world would have enough plugs at some point; it doesn't seem so, though.

-Margaret

I get all my motivational management talk from this book.

Being in charge of a company takes leadership, it takes a certain something that not everyone has. I do though. I have the ability to put across what I want to say in a speech that both motivates and instils fear into my employees. They need to be reminded that I'm in charge and that what I say goes.

I've gone off topic. This book helped me to work out that my boss also has a copy. It also helped me to see that even when talking management talk he talks absolute rubbish. He must be retarded. Or bored. Or both, who knows.

I like to keep things fresh in my company and, by doing so, keep my staff on their toes. I must be good at it because there has never been a drop in profit during the whole thirty years I've been in charge. That says something about a man, that does.

This book helps me to really nail down the points I need to make and introduce my staff to a more professional way of talking when they're on the phone selling the product to new customers. I think I have a pretty strong vision for where we're going as a company. Sometimes explaining it to the idiots I employ can be hard work. Especially Margaret as she is one of those people that know everything already. To be honest I'll be glad when she retires in a few years and I can really get my teeth into the company and fine tune the intricate details of the procedures without her in the way.

I'm looking forward to the next in the series.

Don't let the title put you off. This book is educational and a real tool for any successful director. I wouldn't be without it.

-Mr Hogsbottom

THE DREAM DICTIONARY FROM A TO Z: THE ULTIMATE A-Z TO INTERPRET THE SECRETS OF YOUR DREAMS [PAPERBACK]

Made me realise pulling your own hair out is OK — in a dream.

I just had to buy this book. I keep having dreams about pulling my own hair out. It's disturbing me. I've never really been a dreamer in the past but recently they've been coming thick and fast. They're all different scenarios but in all of them the end result is the same: I pull my hair out.

In the dreams I'm crying because pulling your hair out hurts, be it in dreams or in real life. Seriously, it feels like I've been drugged or something, although I'm not sure what drugs bring on intensely horrible dreams. I looked up the pulling hair thing and apparently it means that I am becoming aware of my own potential. Which I think means I'm really clever. I must have a sick brain, though, I mean what kind of brain would let you know that you're great by making you pull your own hair out?

I've tried grabbing a handful of hair in real life and it really does hurt. It also makes you look mental. I was doing it at my desk one day and Sandy walked past. She jumped, all startled in her pretty little way, then ran off. I had to chase her back to her cubicle and explain that I was just testing what it felt like. I didn't get to tell her why as Mick the security man walked past and told me to stop bothering people and get on with my work. He's not my boss but he *is* bigger than me, so I did as he asked and spent the rest of the week plotting bloody revenge against him. I haven't decided how yet, but I will get him back for embarrassing me in front of Sandy. To make that day worse I lost my book in the process of jogging back to my desk. Not because I was scared of 'Mick' — it was just good exercise. I checked the route several times, but the book wasn't there. Shame, as I also need to look up what it means when you dream about someone you work with all the time. When you're awake.

-Donald

Glad I didn't pay for it.

I found this book on the office floor after I had to tell Donald to leave the office junior alone. I'm surprised he's still got his job here, the way he carries on. Part of my job is to monitor what he's up to and make sure he doesn't get too close to her. Although she doesn't help things by talking to him when she walks past his desk. I think this is out of politeness, though, as the times I've had to send him back to his desk she's looked positively frightened of him.

He'll be gone soon, though, the report I've written for Mr Hogsbottom is pretty damning and I've not had to make anything up either. I normally don't have to do this kind of work, Hogsbottom likes to keep his staff, but Donald has become a particular pain in the last couple of years and although he has been spoken to numerous times, he doesn't listen. There was even suspicion of him putting drugs in the kettle so females would be susceptible to his advances, although we couldn't prove that. I'm looking forward to the day I'm allowed to throw him down the stairs. It's funny, I've never really felt like this before about someone. I'm not sure why I hate him so much, but it's there. Maybe he is just one of those people that invokes hatred in others.

I'm glad I found this book, though, as it explained the dreams I've been having lately. I've been dreaming that I'm running away from something. I'm not sure why I keep having the same nightmare, It's only come on recently, too. I learnt it means that it means I'm anxious. Although I'm not sure I am. So seeing as this book is rubbish I drew a huge penis in the middle pages and chucked it as far away from Donald's cubicle as possible, just so he couldn't find it. This made me feel much better.

-Mick

For thick people who don't understand why they're having nightmares.

I found this on the floor of my office the other day whilst going the long way round to the ladies. Donald, the office pest, was bothering me again so I avoided his desk. I'd seen him trying to pull his own hair out, causing him to chase me, shouting something about nightmares. I was lucky Mick, the security man, stopped him in his tracks or I don't know what I'd have done. It didn't stop him trying to come back, though, he kept creeping up the office trying to continue whatever conversation he thought he was having with me, then slinking back again. Mick was a gem, though, he made him go back every time.

It seems that one of the workers has been having nightmares, although it must be someone thick as there is a reason I've been having nightmares lately and I've not had to spend a tenner on a book to find out why. We've all been eating lots of cheese. The men have been particularly greedy. Well, all except Jeff. He only eats bananas.

-Sandy

OXO GOOD GRIPS BOX GRATER

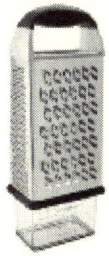

Good, but watch your fingers.

That tight git Hogsbottom ordered too much cheese from one of his internet sites. We all knew he'd brought it, like we always know he's been spending. He has some kind of shopping addiction. There is rarely a day that goes by when he doesn't get a load of parcels delivered right under all our noses. I doubt he even remembers what he's ordered half the time. The only time we see him smile is when he skips out his office once he sees the parcel van pull up. The disappointment on his face when he realises none are for him is something that cheers my morning right up.

The amount of cheese that came was incredible. God knows what he thought he was going to do with it when he ordered it. No doubt he got it cheap, but even so, it's stupid.

It upsets us workers that he'd rather give it away to charity than give his workers a little reward for putting up with each other for so much of our lives. However, he did run out of people who wanted cheese and relented and said we could have it, whilst at work, at lunchtime only.

I was given the task of cutting it all up and putting it on crackers, then putting those crackers on plates, to make sure the staff only had a certain amount each. 'I'm nothing if not fair,' Mr Hogsbottom said, handing me a huge box of cheapo crackers that he'd bought.

By the second day I felt I deserved some cheese for myself for the task of chopping the cheese. Call me selfish but I thought *sod it, I'll have some.*

They were wrapped in 700 gram lumps, so I took five of those home a day for the last three days of the week, although this created problems of its own. I didn't know what to do with it, either. Living alone, there is only so much cheese you can eat, especially when you're on a diet, like I am.

This grater was a life saver. My only word of warning would be that after you've done four blocks, your hands get a bit numb from the pressure and you're likely to slip and grate your hand. That's what happened to me. I had to throw most of the last block I did that night away. I may be fat and eat almost anything, but eating cheese covered in my own blood is going too far even by my standards. I'm not French.

-Margaret

HOW TO DEAL WITH EMOTIONALLY EXPLOSIVE PEOPLE [PAPERBACK]

Doesn't really work on simple people.

You'd think anyone would be happy with a huge card with their favourite band on it for their birthday. Jeff, the office messenger boy, wasn't though. Apparently it wasn't 'mixed' enough for him, whatever the hell that means. How was I supposed to know that Jeff is torn between The Jackson Five and Westlife, so much so that he needs to cut the heads off every poster, picture and T-shirt and switch them about so that each band had equal representation? It's ridiculous!

The scene that followed me presenting him with the well-thought-out gift from all his colleagues was like something out of 'One Flew Over The Cuckoo's Nest'. There was screaming, rocking, self-harm with a ruler. It was awful. All the time he was chanting a weird medley of both The Jackson Five and Westlife's top hits. 'It's as easy as one, two, flying withoooout wiiiings.'

It was the strangest thing I've ever seen.

Since that day Jeff has been rather unkind to me and although he has stopped slapping his own face with a ruler and rocking like someone who's practicing skiing, he has taken to angrily slamming his messaging note pad on my desk when asking if I have messages to send, although he doesn't ask verbally: he has written down 'What?' and that's it. Then he stands there, staring at me as if I just threw his mother down the stairs whilst frantically flattening his strange hair. It's not something I come to work for.

I've tried speaking to the boss, but he's not interested. Jeff is here to stay and regardless of the nice thing I did in buying him a birthday card and a very nice inflatable monkey, Jeff doesn't seem to be able to let his anger go. The only thing I can do is deal with it and hopefully learn some tools as to how to handle him. I bought this book with trepidation, I wondered if a book would really solve my problem.

In a word, no. Unfortunately Jeff wasn't prepared to even try and work things out. Every day I still have to put up with him being an idiot.

What I have learnt, though, is that Jeff is his own man with his own insecurities and his own fears. Fear leads to anger. I think at some point Jeff has been scared of something to do with these bands and this has caused his anger. I pity Jeff now, not that I didn't anyway, he's always been a loser, but now I pity him a bit more for not being able to work through his anger.

I know his father died when he was young, too, but the rumour is that he wasn't a nice person to be around. Bit of a fiddler by all accounts. I've also learnt from this book that Jeff probably hates his father, maybe even for dying and leaving him. Although I don't think his father had anything to do with his own death. No, that was down to one of the husbands of the women in the last factory that he worked in that 'accidentally' drove over him in a freezer truck.

I understand now that other people's anger is not my problem, I don't have to engage in it, that's what they want. I don't hate Jeff in return, either. I did for a while, now I just pray to God that he manages to find a way out of his fear and anger or he'll just continue to have little happiness in his life.

-Margaret

QUIZ MASTER [PAPERBACK]

Good book.

I like to try and keep things fun and friendly in the office. After all, a happy workforce is an easily motivated workforce. I do different things throughout the year, fun things.

Only a few months ago we had a bring your own cake day alongside a jumble sale. Although I have to admit, I did set that up on a Saturday and no one wanted to come in. But, as I said to them, you have to have fun and if that takes someone pushing a little bit to make that happen so be it. I think they all enjoyed it. Donald certainly got loads out of it, he was rushing around carrying all of Sandy's stuff for her. He even bought most of it, too. She made an absolute killing. Margaret was a miserable swine all day, as expected. She's dead wood to this company, just sitting there waiting for me to let her go home and not have to come back in anymore while getting free money off the Government, just for being old. Everyone else seemed to love it though.

I also managed to shift most of my old shirts to Jeff and all the other things my wife decided I wasn't allowed to own anymore, which was kind of the whole point of having the event. I would have done it in the name of Blue Peter; however, they told me at the age of forty-five I would need a child involved and I don't have one of them. I thought about using Jeff for a little while but realized his hairstyle would be a dead give away as to his age if anyone checked, so I just thought I'd donate the profits, and by profits I mean the ones everyone else made (I spent mine on cigars) to the local hospital. It went well and I managed to get the company a little PR and I'm sure next time the hospital need some bath plugs they'll remember the day that Hogsbottom Plugs were there in their hour of need, holding a massive cheque for the amount of £32.64.

I love quizzes and always used to win them when I was allowed to go to the pub on my own. I'm not now, though. An unfortunate incident involving the pub's Jack Russell and two bottles of Courvoisier put paid to that. The dog's OK now, though, if a little mentally scarred. It was hands down that a quiz would be the next team building activity for the team here at Hogsbottom Plugs.

I decided it would be fun to recreate the quiz atmosphere at work. Sorting all the questions out didn't take long. Basically I just ripped out three or four pages from different places in the book, then the matching answer pages, and photo copied the lot. Easy.

The questions all seemed fairly mixed. Some hard, some easy. I had to cater for everyone. That's another thing about being a boss, you need to make sure everyone can achieve their best and feel good about doing it. The hard ones I had in mind for Mark, he's done so much in his life I'm sure they will be something he can excel in. The easier ones are for Donald and Jeff. All they seem to have done, or in fact, do, is work for me then go home again. I suspect they'll both get at least one question right. I've asked people to write their name on the answers sheet and I'll give a point for everyone who gets it right. It'll be like a joke, but I suspect Donald will get nothing other than that. Jeff will get the music questions, too. His mum told me that he's really into The Jackson Five and Westlife, so I've picked a couple of them. Margaret will no doubt try to sabotage things, but won't be able to stop herself answering the questions on cooking; she sees herself as the office Jamie Oliver. I just mixed the others up as they're a mixed bunch and all seem to be able to get to work on time without getting run over, so I was sure they'd be fine without hand-picked questions.

THE OFFICE IDIOT REVIEWS

I was right: as expected, Mark wiped the floor with everybody. And that was without going to the toilet and checking hidden encyclopaedias as some suggested he might. There seems to be a rumour going round that Mark is a bit of a tell-tale, a bit of a liar. I think all sour grapes, though, because Mark knows more than they ever could. In his interview I was absolutely blown away by his wealth of experience in so many different walks of life. You name it, Mark's done it or walked out from it. How he settled on health and safety, I don't know. But I'm lucky he did and him winning the quiz just underlines that point.

I made sure that there was no popping into the lavs to check phones or the aforementioned encyclopaedias. Mick, the head of security, rigged up a couple of cameras and was on the look out for anyone using phones, laptops or books. He runs a tight ship security wise and the quiz was no different.

I enjoy standing in front of my team, being the centre of attention. I wanted to keep things fun so I did my impression of the guy who introduces the X Factor contestants. Although after everybody shouted out 'What?' I stopped and went for the even funnier high pitched voice, they all loved that.

Mark was pleased with his prize of the rest of the afternoon off. I know it was Saturday, but at least he didn't have to stay behind and put all the tables back.

A good time was had by all, all thanks to me, and of course this book.

-Mr Hogsbottom

FRIEDLAND RESPONSE CA5 PROFESSIONAL HEAVY DUTY WIRED COLOUR CCTV CAMERA KIT

Heavy duty anti-dogging camera.

Cameras and covert filming are my speciality. I've been interested in filming for as long as I can remember. I recently decided to get a proper job instead of uploading silly videos to YouTube.

My first task didn't disappoint. I had to buy a new camera. The big cheese, Mr Hogsbottom, called me the other day, there'd been complaints that people are using the side of the factory for doing things that he doesn't pay them to do. Having sex. Although if the rumours are true he does pay some of the factory girls for that. He's a hot head and when it comes to the 'name of the company' being dragged into the dirt, he's prepared to spend a little money and stamp his feet a little. Hence I had to buy this camera and spend almost a full day setting it up and splicing it into the current, already huge, CCTV network of the company.

Until I got out there, I thought it was just another office rumour, there is always rumours of so and so dilly-dallying about this person or that person. Although the amount of used condoms I got John the cleaner to pick up proved that there had been something fishy going on.

I'll soon see who it is, though, the camera is up and working now. It's night and day so there'll be no hiding from it.

-Mick

FOAM CERVICAL COLLAR NECK SUPPORT / BRACE MEDIUM

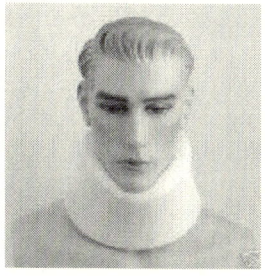

Helps gain compensation.

Every day is like every other in the office where I work. Nothing changes too much. I've had my desk since I've been here, I've used the same pen for ten years, it's just a bit mundane. Although I would rather have mundane than the pain I'm in now. I got to work as normal the other day. When things are always the same, when something out of the ordinary happens it is all the more a shock. I sat in my chair and it just fell apart. I ended up on the floor in a heap of my own arms and legs and at least six different parts of the chair. I hit the floor with a bump and immediately knew I'd jarred my neck.

    No one helped, even Mark, the health and safety officer, walked past and did nothing. He was too busy telling someone on the end of his phone that he was running a double marathon at the weekend. I've since asked him to come and see me so we can get a report filled out, but he still hasn't. I doubt he even knows what the form is. His idea of health and safety is walking round in a hard hat, pointing to wires and telling us to 'sort them'. It was this attitude that made me decide that I would be suing the company. Hopefully it'll bring my retirement age closer. Yes, it meant demanding an ambulance and sitting in A&E for ages, but I read in one of my magazines a few years ago that you get extra on a claim if you do that.

I could have sworn Jeff was laughing when it happened. The evil little swine. I decided to leave the label of this neck brace (that the NHS made me pay for) out just to upset him. Which worked. He saw it and ran off straight through the cubicle walls, almost knocking Sandy over. The place was a right tip. I've got my fingers crossed Hogsbottom will be taking the money for new walls out of Jeff's wages.

The only plus is that I get to take the painkillers and forget I've been to work; I'd be surprised if I remember writing this.

-Margaret

FCUK FRENCH CONNECTION CONNECT HIM EAU DE TOILETTE SPRAY FOR MEN 100ML

Good for pulling hot birds!

Being a tower of attraction to woman is something I've had to put up with throughout my life. It's a gift *and* a burden. School, college, work — everywhere. Mostly, I love it. I know deserve it, even, for being such a good bloke.

You can imagine my surprise when last week a woman I was seeing at work suddenly broke things off and refused to keep coming round the side of the factory with me for my lunchtime conjugals. The excuse she gave of 'just not feeling like it' doesn't wash with me, she'd been like a raging nympho for a couple of weeks before that, coming to find me, dragging *me* round the back. Then just stopped. I'm not having that. I'm the one who does the dumping. Never, never, the other way round. I've brought this aftershave in an attempt to a) get some more lunchtime fun going, and b) put me back in a position to be the one that dumps her. That'll show her.

Women love nice-smelling men. I know this as the adverts all say it, so it must be true.

I was surprised at Margaret's reaction to me spraying this in and around her cubicle. My plan was to get her used to the smell so she'd fall in love with it, then when I wafted past just before lunch, she'd be back to her old ways and be following me down the back stairs without even being asked. All I got was a torrent of abuse and then the sight of Margaret chucking up in her bin.

I admit that maybe I shouldn't have put on half a bottle and then sprayed a bit over the top of the cubicle just before I walked in, but how was I to know she was eating and had her mouth open?

Back to the drawing board. It does smell nice though. I'd suggest just a couple of sprays, though, as I got called a 'perfume ponce' on the bus that night.

-Mark

SENOKOT MAX STRENGTH 24 TABLETS

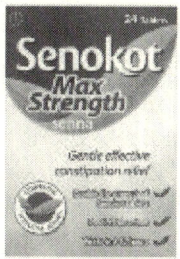

Helps digest my diet of bananas and bananas.

With all the bananas I eat things get a little blocked up from time to time. Mum bought me these to help things along. I suppose if you only eat one type of food it will lead to this problem, but not having to deal with the texture of other foods is worth the pain of clearing the decks on a weekly basis.

I use the ladies' toilet as the men's is just uncouth. The grunts and the talking on the phone can really put me off my stride. I can hear some of the clenching and groaning over my earphones, that's how loud it is. The women's is much quieter and relaxing. It has a certain ambience to it, too. The women always spray a little perfume once they've been, too, which only adds to the mood needed to pass the week's worth of bananas and get back to my important job of chief messenger.

I normally keep these little saviours in my desk; however, recently someone stole them. I think it was Margaret, the receptionist. She's recently become something of a pain after I informed her that under no circumstances should Westlife or The Jackson Five be represented on their own on anything gifted or, in fact, shown to me. It's not something I can or will put up with. Since her reaction to this news, I've not been able to look her in the eye. She can't be the nice person I thought she was. Imagine someone buying you a birthday card with just one of your favourite bands on? She must know I can't bring myself to choose between them. That's why I have my mix and match heads T-shirts. I'm not happy with her. Plus I've got to buy more of these, which is affecting my gold fund.

I don't like spending money on anything other than gold and the merchandise of Westlife and The Jackson Five. They're all one and the same, investments. They'll all make me money one day, then I'll be able to buy the house me and Mum live in, just as Dad would have if he hadn't died.

On the whole, I'm glad I've got these, but not happy I had to pay extra for the replacements out of my own money. I mean, what is the DLA my mum gets supposed to be spent on? These. That's what.

-Jeff

COCCYX POSTURE CHAIR WITH VISCO MEMORY FOAM GREAT FOR THE OFFICE

The most uncomfortable chair I have ever perched on.

After weeks of waiting for my boss, Mr Hogsbottom, and the health and safety officer, Mark, to sort things out, they've finally presented me with this beast. I'm not sure what they were thinking. I asked for a chair, not a torture device. After my last chair collapsed from under me I had to have a meeting about my weight. I know I'm big boned, but I'm not big enough for a chair I've been sitting on for years to just fall apart one day. It must have been faulty. Mark seems to think different, though, and after I put a claim in for the injury to my neck and back, he decided I needed to get this chair to help me not hurt myself further.

    I was distraught when I walked in and saw this thing sitting where my chair used to go. There was no budging them and because I've been putting on the neck and back pain there was no way out of sitting on this. When I tried to argue, Mark just said, 'Oh, I thought you needed to support your back?' In a sly way. The evil swine. He enjoyed seeing me trying to get on this for the first time. Although he wasn't about to see me fall off this and caught me when I tried to slip off. That caused him to pull me into the meeting room and give me a full morning's training on this chair and how to use it. I then needed to sign something to say I was happy I had been shown how to use it.

    I feel like a right tit perched on this, it's higher than all the other chairs and my head pokes over the partition walls of my cubicle. Everyone can just see my head popping over the wall when they're walking about.

It's not even comfortable. I get a bad back after a day sitting on this. It's only been a week and I'm not used to it at all.

The no win, no claim company reckon I'll get about five grand for the claim, I'm starting to wonder if It's all worth it. I've tried swapping the chair and sitting on one from the staff room, but Mark keeps coming by and demanding I use the new one.

If you actually have a bad back this might help; however, if you're faking one, I'm not sure this chair is for you. If you are going to pretend to have an injury, I think it would be better to choose the legs, that way you'd get a nice little foot stool rather than this thing.

-Margaret

SILVERLINE HANDY SPONGES 3PK

These soak up everything!

I had to buy ten of these! The office I work in is placed next to a factory that went out of business a few years ago, since when people have been dumping anything and everything in the grounds. It's become quiet unhygienic to say the least. Not only do we have rats running about, viewable from the office window, but we have flocks, and I mean FLOCKS, of seagulls circling overhead. There are hundreds of the little devils. It's not something anyone wants to get used to, but we have to. I've complained to Mr Hogsbottom more times than I care to remember and every time — nothing. He wouldn't care as he parks his car in the factory and doesn't have to walk under them and risk getting his head pecked or pooed on.

Last week something tragic happened. I was just looking out the window wishing it was time to go home when I saw the biggest and runniest seagull poo I've ever laid eyes on slop itself onto the office window, then another, then another. The whole flock were dropping dirty bombs against the office. It seemed as though we were under attack in some new form of poo warfare. Sandy, the office junior, was the only one brave enough to go to the window at first. Although once we'd all seen the shocked look on her face, we were soon behind her. The scene outside was like nothing I've ever seen before. The seagulls must have been in distress or something, because they all had a severe case of the trots. There was a river of white just falling out the sky. They were all screaming more than normal, too. The vehicles in the car park were absolutely covered in it.

I mean, you couldn't make out what colour they were.

Mark, the health and safety officer, started telling one of his stories about how he'd seen this before and thought it was mating season or something. Which just made the sight of what we were seeing weirder, to be honest.

God only knows what the poor birds had eaten, but more than a few of them were literally dropping out the sky and dying from diarrhoea. We managed to see it for about ten minutes; however, after that all the windows were white and we couldn't see out of them.

All we could do was watch the disaster unfold until the windows were completely blacked out with white seagull poop.

The squealing eventually stopped and after looking for (and not finding) Mark and the cleaner, John, we had to decide who was going to stick their head outside the door first. Unfortunately for Donald, we picked him unanimously. And although he wasn't as keen as the rest of us were for him to go outside, after a bit of verbal persuasion from me and a physical shove from Mick, the head of security, Donald was outside. Not for long, mind. He was soon back inside and completely covered in the smelly white slime. Turns out he'd slipped on one of the fallen birds and landed in a pool of the stuff. Although it didn't stop the birds on the roof dropping a few more dirty bombs into his face and hair as he clambered back to his feet. Needless to say he wouldn't go back out for a second look once he'd got himself clean, a process that seemed to take longer than a shower should. I have my suspicions he was crying.

It took a call to the fire brigade and then the council before anyone who may have been able to help turned up. First it was the fire brigade, then environmental health, and then, finally, the RSPB, who scattered some sort of special medicine feed across the tip next door, then we had to sit and wait a further three hours while it worked on the birds that hadn't done themselves dead. Our cars were un-drivable so they had to take us home in a mini bus borrowed from some day centre. I've never travelled in a sunshine bus before, I can't say the same

THE OFFICE IDIOT REVIEWS

for some of the other members of staff though. We were promised by the chaps from environmental health that the cars would be hosed down by them before they left.

Of course, though, they were from the council so there was no lie too big to tell. When we got there in the morning, half a job of hosing down the driveway had been done. That was it.

I had to use the sponges from the cleaning ladies' broom cupboard and go out and do my own car, and unfortunately I used all the sponges we had, so Donald and Mick had to risk driving to the car wash. No doubt it was man somewhere along the line who was to blame.

These are the replacements. They must be good quality as the cleaning lady hasn't noticed. Maybe I should write to the council and suggest they use these.

-Margaret

NAVIR LOOKY PERISCOPE

Works, but not very inconspicuous.

I'm just so depressed. Life is terrible, I work in a rubbish job, have no girlfriend, a terrible company car and don't get to go train spotting as often as I'd like. Everyone in the office hates me. Well, almost everyone. Sandy, the office junior, talks to me. I like her, too. In fact I'm a little obsessed by her. It's the only pleasure I get — thinking about her. I often spend my days wondering what it would be like if we were together.

The amount of time I think about us being together for varies. Sometimes it's just five minutes in the office toilets; in other, longer, fantasies, we get married and are together forever. It makes the days go a little quicker. Sometimes I wonder if I should tell her. I mean, she does speak to me, it must mean she is interested on some level, mustn't it? Although there is always the risk she won't talk to me anymore. Then I'll be left on my own in my cubicle all day with only my Red Bull and sleeping pills to take away the pain of being me. Honestly, since they got rid of all the tea ladies in British offices, I reckon there's been more lonely people in the world.

The problem I have is that Sandy isn't around as much as I'd like her to be, one or two conversations a day isn't enough. Especially as the second always seems to be started by me and she either doesn't seem interested or Mick from security takes it upon himself to send me back to my own desk. I decided I wasn't going to keep starting them, my brain couldn't take the rejection.

THE OFFICE IDIOT REVIEWS

Now, there's only so much time you can spend hovering about reception watching Sandy on the CCTV. When Margaret's there, she moans like hell if I hang about too long. She thinks I'm weird and isn't shy about telling me so. I'm not sure she realises that I'm staring at the monitor behind her; the camera near the door points over Sandy's desk so I can get a really good look at her there. I like looking at her.

Margaret moaning about me hovering motivated me to find a different solution. At first I thought about getting my own camera set up. However, the cost and the fact I have no idea how to set one up put me off that idea. That's when I came across this little beauty.

I practiced using it at home. Unfortunately there isn't a zoom on it, but I could make out the TV from the hallway. If I ever get rich I might pay someone to invent a digital periscope.

So, hiding the periscope in a kitchen roll holder, I prepared myself for the office. I was so excited. I took it in on a Friday and all I have to do on Fridays is a couple of Excel sheets, meaning I could spend the rest of the day looking at Sandy.

It didn't go too well. The people in my office are such prudes. Jeff, the office simpleton, believed I was looking into a homemade kaleidoscope and maybe with hindsight I was silly to base the rest of the afternoon's activities on Jeff buying my story. The lens was trained on Sandy and I got a full view of her face when she turned round. What happened, it turns out, is that Sandy had seen the end of the periscope poking out the end of the tube. A schoolboy error, you might think, but I had to see out of it didn't I?

Sandy told Mark, Mark told Mick, and Mick came and snatched away my periscope and physically dragged me out my cubicle and into the meeting room. With the blinds pulled, either Mark or Mick punched me in the ribs a couple of times, but stopped when I wailed.

Mr Hogsbottom has suspended me for a week while there is an investigation. I was marched to the bus stop and watched getting on a bus. I couldn't even take the car or say goodbye to Sandy.

Now I need something to do for this week off work. There's no way it will be longer, I hope not anyway, I'm not sure I can manage without seeing Sandy for longer than that. I better subscribe to an extra TV channel or two.

-Donald

RUDDINGS WOOD 25KG WILD BIRD SEED/BIRD FOOD

Seagulls like these with a little seasoning.

It was high time I really showed Margaret who was boss in the office, in fact all of them. They think I'm just some silly little boy who takes their messages and is solely there to be poked fun at. Well, this 'little boy' had had enough. Watching YouTube, I saw a video that really stood out and along with the laxatives I already had, this bird seed was all I needed.

I started by mixing the laxatives with water, adding a couple of bottles of my mum's heavy duty stuff just to make sure it all worked. Then I simply poured the mush all over the seeds and left them to ferment in my dad's old shed. I popped back over the next week to give it all a stir and make sure the seeds were keeping their form. Once the seeds had sucked up all the liquid I started to bag the mixture up.

Now, I knew that John, the cleaner, and Mark, the health and safety manager, were running a scam on the refuse collection. Rather than pay the council the rates a business needs to, they've been pocketing the company's money and then slinging the bags over into the disused factory next door. This caused vermin. Rats, pigeons and, more than anything, seagulls. These were my weapons. They eat anything. When the day came I went round the building carefully placing the bags of soggy seed in the bins, then sat and waited until just before lunchtime, which is when John goes round collecting all the sacks. It couldn't have gone better. He didn't suspect a thing All I had to do was wait. The seeds did kick up a stink so it wouldn't be long before the gulls would be down.

Unfortunately the gulls took a little longer than expected to get their nostrils onto the seeds and everyone was back from lunch by the time they were circling. Although the sheer amount that showed up was more than I've ever seen before, even at the beach. I don't know if they sent one of the pigeons they bullied off the rubbish pile to tell all their mates or what, but they certainly have some way of telling each other there is food aplenty. That much was clear.

It was only after about ten minutes that the first of the many drone attacks slopped into the office window. SPLAT. Right near Margaret's stupid, fat face. It startled her so much she jumped. After the first one it was like the plug had been pulled on a bath as it started raining white. Everyone ran over to the window to see what was going on; there was turned up noses, gasps, people hand-wringing and most of all Margaret standing there dumbfounded as her car was pounded, along with all the other cars, with slimy white seagull poo. I just put on my headphones and listened to a Jackson Five vs. Westlife power dance ballad.

If I hadn't acted when I did, I would have turned out like my cousin, Brian, who is constantly mocked every time he leaves his house. I'm not as stupid as him, though. This bird seed was totally worth every penny. I am so pleased with how well it worked out. And even though no one knows 'the day the drones attacked', as I've come to call it, was down to me, it makes me feel better just knowing that Margaret got her just desserts for waving her label at me and insulting my choice of music.

I wish I'd saved some seed to be honest. I'd love to see it again. It's a shame I can't get my hands on the CCTV or I'd upload it.

-Jeff

WIZARD WIG AND BEARD LONG WHITE

Made me feel like Jesus for a while.

I've been off work for three days now, which is longer than I'm used to not seeing Sandy, the office junior for. I don't like it. The weekends are bad enough. I just about make it through those two long days by battering my sausage more than a fish shop owner with OCD. I ordered this the evening I got sent home from work, as there was no way I was going to be able to not look at Sandy's lovely face for a whole week. This disguise would help me see her, I hoped I'd even be able to sit next to her on the bus and look. I wouldn't be able to talk to her as she'd know my voice, but I would be able to look; that's all I need.

The delivery was slow, that's something I'm not happy about. If there was an option for next day I would have opted for it, and been happy to pay for it, but there wasn't. The seller needs to take note of the fact that some people, like me, might need this item faster than other people and at least offer the service. It's not like they wouldn't get paid for it, is it?

Using the wig was easy, it's just a slip over the head affair. I loved the feel of it, although I couldn't help wishing it was Sandy's hair I was stroking and not my fake beard. It did make it through the night without being soiled with any bodily fluids though, which was more luck than judgement.

I tested it during the morning. I just nipped to the shop to buy a paper, I always buy a paper. I cut out and collect the

Page 3 pics, but the guy working there didn't notice it was me. He's not the most talkative person in the world, but still, it was good enough for me.

Later I caught the bus into town. (I had to take the bus as my car seemed to have got an infestation of maggots.) I headed down the tow path and waited for Sandy. It was great feeling, being anonymous. I felt a freedom I suspect is only known to superheroes and people who wear anoraks. Hovering round the stairs that lead up to the bus stop I waited ... admittedly I was three hours early, but I wanted to make sure I didn't miss her. That would have completely ruined the whole day. I couldn't bear another night in front of the TV on my own with no recent 'brain pictures' of Sandy. I entertained myself by practicing my hobby of hopping though. I almost managed my record of nine hundred hops without falling over, unfortunately I fell over at eight hundred and eighty three, I think it was the excitement of getting so close that put me off.

Right on time my colleagues all left work, I was ready and waiting at the bus stop, pretending to read the timetable.

To my disappointment, Sandy was with Margaret. They seemed to be huddled together talking out the sides of their mouths.

'You've been told, Donald, stay the F away from us,' Margaret shouted at me before they both hurried past.

It was then I looked down and realised I was wearing the clothes that I always wear; well, I've only got one set. That was how they knew it was me. Not the wig.

-Donald

WILLOW SCREEN FENCE PACK — 1.8 X 1.8M

Exactly what I needed to keep birds out.

I've decided to block off access to the factory next door. I can't have a repeat of the seagull attack we had last week. It's taken my staff that long to scrape it all up. Well, that's a lie, actually. It's taken me almost that long to get them to come back in and start cleaning it up.

I only had Jeff and the new guy, Brian, in for three days and between them they drank all the hot chocolate out the machine and as far as I can make out spent the week dancing in the kitchen rather than doing any work. It was nice to see Jeff and his cousin getting on so well and enjoying themselves, though. Jeff's mum made sure I was rewarded for bringing a friend in for Jeff. He's been really angry lately, ever since Margaret got him the wrong birthday present. He wasn't even cutting his hair properly and it was starting to look a bit of a state and this was causing the kids on the bus to take the mickey more than they usually do.

Anyway, these fence panels seem to have done the trick. I've put several on top of each other and placed spikes on the top so the gulls won't be able to sit there. I've done both sides of the car park just in case Mr Cork's biscuit factory goes the same way as the empty one next door and more vermin starts moving in. I've then got a tightly knitted net and had that put up so my factory and its grounds are vermin-free zones. I've given Mick, the security man, license to shoot any bird that manages to make it past the defences with his secret catapult, usually reserved for firing maggots at Donald's car when the window is left open a crack. Seeing as he's gone and won't be coming back, Mick needs a new use for the catapult.

The panels are sturdy and with the huge posts that Mick used to keep them attached to each other they are doing the job they were bought for. I'd have got Mark to give it the once-over, in fact with all the experience he has at building things due to his time working on the Duchy estate putting footings in for elaborate chicken huts, he'd have been perfect for the job, but he couldn't come in as he was doing some undercover work for the police that weekend.

If you need a fence these are perfect, I've not a bad word to say about them.

-Mr Hogsbottom

MEN'S HEMATITE GLASS ROSARY NECKLACE IN A GIFT BOX

What every new sheep needs.

I think God is repaying me for ripping off the company I work for and the council. Mark, the health and safety guy, offered me some money to cancel the regular refuse pick ups and to, instead, chuck all the rubbish into the disused factory next door. The way he saw it was that it was more money for us and the new owners, whoever they were, were going to have to pay someone to come and shift all the old stuff out the factory and pick up the needles the junkies leave in the outhouses, so we may as well give them something to really clean up and earn some cash in the process. There's also been some monstrous toilet logs that have gone the same way as the bin bags.

Last week there was a strange seagull poo attack on the building. I've never seen anything like it. The whole of the front of the building, the roof, the cars, everything outside was covered completely in seagull mess. On top of that most of the birds died and fell to the ground and made even more of a mess.

While it was happening I was forced to run out the back door and go straight home. I knew it was me who'd get the task of cleaning it up. I wasn't too interested in that.

There's no way it can be anything other than Karma and retribution from God for the evil I've been doing by throwing the rubbish and logs. I mean, what else could cause such a catastrophe?

Hopefully if I can start doing something to rebalance

Karma then I won't have to be a cleaner and deal with turds, I could get a better job, maybe as a priest or work in a car wash or something. It starts with these beads. If I wear them, pray with them, and start reading the Bible while holding them, then I reckon God will see to it that I'm returned to 'being allowed in' status.

I carry these everywhere with me. Work, home, toilet, on the bus — everywhere. I pray at least five times a day. When I get up I offer myself to God and let him know that I'm here to serve him. I also remind him I am sorry for what I did.

I've made the times coincide with my toilet breaks, it's the perfect place as I can lean on the bowl. Although I learnt the hard way to kneel down before I've done what I need to do or I'm just leaning into the stench. Another tip if you're thinking of doing the same, don't go into the cubicle and expect a holy praying experience if you've just seen the fattest bloke in the office exiting on fish and chips Friday. I also have a quick 'up and down' before I leave the building to go home. Just in case God sends the seagulls of death while I'm outside.

When at home I keep the beads in a little case on top of my TV. Sitting above, I've got a little bit of a shrine to Jesus (God's son). It's only a couple of candles and a picture I borrowed from the church when I popped down there to see what it's all about. The vicar was staggering about drunk up at the altar end so he didn't notice. I'm using it for good so I'm sure God doesn't mind a bit.

So far so good, the seagulls haven't been back.

-John the cleaner

CLEARBLUE DIGITAL PREGNANCY TEST KIT WITH CONCEPTION INDICATOR — TWIN-PACK

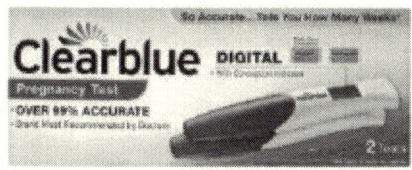

Accurate.

I must have been out my mind to have done it, but I did. I think it must have been the elation of not having to deal with Donald anymore. Or maybe I just noticed that he wasn't the only man in the office who had his eye on me. I'm not a slag or anything, but every woman likes a bit of male attention, don't they?

A few weeks ago, on the day Donald got sent home, Mark was swanning about like he always does, and I ignored him like I always do. However I did notice he was wearing a new scent and I'm a sucker for a man who smells good. Later, we all went to the pub to celebrate Donald not bringing the place down with his misery and weirdness anymore. We all just enjoyed being able to talk about him without having to go in the next day and pretend we hadn't all been out without him. I got carried away and when Mark offered me a lift home I knew what we'd end up doing and I was right.

He wasn't something I'd go back for seconds to. He had an immensely hairy body and the ginger hair made me feel like I was bouncing up and down on an ugly orangutan. He was grinning like one too, it almost put me off my stride. If it hadn't been so long since my last liaison I'd not have had a happy ending at all.

When I woke up in the ginger monkey's bed I felt like my

world had ended. It smelt terrible in there. It was all coming from him. The bed was riddled with a smell that can only be described as a mixture of urine, old tea bags and biscuits.

We didn't use protection. I know, I know. First rule of sleeping around is not to sleep with gingers. The second, use protection. What can I say? I'm a rule breaker.

I'm terrified. The last thing I want is a ginger child. I couldn't love it. Especially not a hairy one that looks like a round-faced monkey. I've been to the chemist and taken a morning after pill, but then Google told me that not all morning after pills work. I've ordered these tests on subscription so that I can check for the next three months. I just need to be sure I'm not due an even bigger mistake than I already have.

Mark keeps on trying to get me on my own again, I think he truly believes he's found the person that isn't going to dump him this time. To such an extent that I could tell him to his face that I hated him, and indeed have, and he'd just walk off saying he'd call me later.

I've had the small problem of getting rid of the tests once I've done them, I can't do them at home as my housemate would be unbearable if she knew I'd slept with a man that has a silly name for his equipment. So I can't risk leaving a bit of the wrapper lying around or anything. The only place to do it is work; however, that brings problems of its own as Mark is in charge of the cleaner, John. And I don't trust either of them. There was no way John would have kept things quiet if he found a used pregnancy test in the rubbish.

So carrying a urine soaked stick, albeit a digital one, round the office in my pocket was the only solution. Unfortunately on one of these occasions Jeff had just seen the label of Margaret's neck brace again and was motoring along the corridor, head down, trying to get away as quick as possible. I was just turning into the office. He whacked straight into me and sent me and everything I was carrying flying into one of the cubicle walls, which did as good a job of holding me up as a piece of tissue paper. Seriously, they're worse than those hospital curtains that the whole NHS seems to think are soundproof. It also caused one wall to fall into another. This set off the domino effect and one by one they all fell over. I was so embarrassed, I just got myself up quickly and did a bit of head down, motoring off of my own while plastering a 'what happened?' look on my face.

It was only when Mark started waving the test round whilst inspecting the damage (and telling people that he used to be an assessor for an insurance company) that I realized I must have dropped it in the collision. I had to come clean when he asked. I hate lying. I just can't do it. I told Mark that I was worried about being pregnant. Of course he asked if I'd done a test. I completely came clean about having no periods and being constipated recently.

He won't leave me alone now and has even been round to the house and told my housemate. I know it's bad, but I've got to make him out to be a liar. But he's ginger and smells like a monkey, so it's his own fault if you think about it.

-Sandy

PREGNANCY FOR MEN: THE WHOLE NINE MONTHS [PAPERBACK]

Everything in here except how to make someone love you.

I was lucky enough to get a night with the office hottie. I'm not sure, but I may be even luckier that she's now pregnant. I suppose it is lucky, if you think about, it as we'll be linked for life and I'm bound to get the chance to give her another go on my ding-a-ling-a-do-dah. I'm keen on that.

This book is great, it gives all the information we need at this special time of foetal development. It's all set out in easy to understand stages — there are three, in case you're interested. It also gives suggestions on how to deal with the woman during this time. However, there is one problem; the book doesn't tell you how to deal with a woman who keeps ignoring you and pretending you didn't sleep together.

I'm not sure how to get round it. I've been going over to her at work, just offering her a drink or a sit down. I even brought one of those portable chairs for that very reason, but she just marches off swearing. Not one to be put off by a bad mood, I popped round her house and knocked on the door, I thought she'd been funny as she didn't want everyone to know that she'd succumbed to the office stud, but when I got there she wouldn't even come to the door, she just screamed something obscene through the letter box and left me outside. When her housemate returned to find me sitting near the bins,

THE OFFICE IDIOT REVIEWS

I tried to explain to that I was waiting for Sandy, but she simply wouldn't believe that we were boyfriend and girlfriend. She just sneered and walked off calling me a ginger moron. It's pretty soul destroying, really. She didn't need to add the ginger part.

It hasn't stopped me reading the book, though. It explains that woman can be fairly up and down in the first three months when their hormones are all over the place. I've just got to be patient and let her come to terms with the fact that her life is going to change and her body is going to grow everywhere (brilliant).

I'll keep reading the book so I can support Sandy.

I can't wait to be a father, I've told all my friends on Facebook and even posted a picture I took of Sandy at work to show the kind of sort that I've managed to impregnate. Everyone's impressed. Well, they've never pulled something as hot as Sandy. Although Barry's comment that 'the picture looked like it was taken without her knowing' was a little too close to the truth. I removed it so as not to lower my social standing.

-Mark

NINTENDO 3DS HANDHELD CONSOLE

Great for boredom.

Enough is enough, there are too many logs being dropped in the toilet that I'm responsible for cleaning. It's just getting too much. Every other day I'm having to fish something ungodly out of the pan and get rid of it. It wasn't so bad when I could just chuck them over to next door, but unfortunately after we were all punished for that, It's not something I'm risking again. The seagull attack was terrible.

I decided I was going to catch whoever was doing it and ordered this to give myself something to do while waiting. I chose the brain training game. I figured that if I was going to potentially spend all day sitting in the female toilets I should at least get something (other than a sense of being a pervert) out of it.

The unit itself is easy to get going. Pretty much just switch it on and you're ready to go. The brain training game was a little taxing, though; I kept wondering how they justified letting kids play it. My first go told me I had the mind of an eight year old, then things went downhill from there, the more I tried. I can't imagine a child finding this game very uplifting.

The worst part about this purchase was that I didn't charge it before I took it into the toilet, so it only lasted an hour then I had nothing to do except sit there waiting for the culprit. It definitely needs to come charged, right out the box.

I sat there for almost four hours before I got bored and left with no more idea of who was causing the problem than when I went in.

THE OFFICE IDIOT REVIEWS

I did learn one thing though: woman fart louder than men when they're in the toilet and some laugh to themselves after, too. Most spray perfume if they've done anything more than that. I felt like I was walking through the Boots' perfume section at one particularly busy time. It's amazing how many women have the same body clock in my office.

I didn't even hear any gossip that I didn't already know, either.

-John the cleaner

CATERING CLING FILM

Clings well.

I've had enough of the huge toilet logs now. I tried putting a notice up about it, a polite one too. It stated:

'I'm not angry, but there have been some incredibly large stools in the pan recently. They are too big too flush away and yours truly has had to remove them by hand. It's not what I get out of bed in the morning for. Could whoever is doing it please, PLEASE, try and break them mid-way a couple of times. Just to get them round the U-bend. Thank you, John.'

It didn't work, though, within hours someone had dropped not one, but two, in different pans. Someone had also written 'Ha ha' on my posters and added a smiley face, too.

Outraged was an understatement. It was seeing the blatent mocking of me that gave me an idea. Whoever it is is invading my work space with logs so I would do the same. I got the two offending sticks of everything that is wrong with humanity, stuck them on a plate and wrapped them in this clingfilm. I then placed them centre stage in the office fridge with a copy of my note clearly visable to all who opened the door.

Of course I had to deny all knowledge when Mark, the health and safety officer, and Mr Hogsbottom, the MD, called me into the office to discuss 'my stress levels'. Lying didn't work, though. I'd forgotten I signed the note.

I've lost my job now. It was worth it, though, as I don't have to deal with toilets anymore. Or their contents. Hardly anyone else in my village works so I won't be an outcast.

-John the cleaner

MINI PORTABLE 4L FRIDGE FOR GIFT, CAR FRIDGE, MINI PORTABLE 4L FRIDGE FOR GIFT

Good for separating your lunch from the office weirdos.

The office that I work in seems to be going downhill. First I was stalked by one of the longest-term salesmen. Then I go to get my lunch out the fridge and the cleaner had put a plate of poo in there, all wrapped up in clingfilm. It was disgusting. I was so hungry too. Being pregnant has turned me into a right pig where food's concerned. Well, when my stomach isn't churning at the thought of what the baby might look like. (Her father is a really hairy and smelly.)

This little fridge is great as I can keep it under my desk. It holds all my lunch and I also fill it with other treats to keep me going throughout the day. The only thing I have to say negatively about it is that if you put a can of drink in there you can't fit in as many treats.

I'm hoping that now Donald the stalker and John the dirty cleaner are gone, things will get a little better round here.

-Sandy

FUJIFILM FINEPIX S2980 DIGITAL CAMERA (14MP, 18X OPTICAL ZOOM) 3 INCH LCD SCREEN

Cheap and looks expensive.

What with all the changes that have been going on recently, things have been a little unsettled around the office. I've had to get rid of two staff in as many weeks. Before this I'd never sacked anyone, ever. Unfortunately, in the days of internet and free lawyers there is just no way I can get away with 'having a quiet word' with staff who stalk others and ones that put toilet mess in the fridge. It's a shame as in the olden days I'm pretty sure I could have sorted these issues with an inspirational staff meeting.

To make everyone feel a little bit better and stop anymore of them leaving, I managed to get a visit from our local MP, Elouise Munch. She agreed to come and officially open the new dining area. I set aside the area that used to be Donald's desk as an eating area. All the chairs set out nicely and so on.

Elouise opened the new eating area, she talked rubbish, and tried to get my staff to vote for her in the election. Best of all, though, she allowed me to take a photograph of her with the team all enjoying the spread I'd laid on (cheese) sandwiches. We were all under strict instructions to wear our best outfits. Jeff put his best shoes on and even agreed to put one of my jackets on over his two T-shirts and shirt. We all stood beaming for the camera. Just before the shot was taken, Brian, the new guy, shouted 'Smile if you think Mr Hogsbottom is the best boss in the world!'

The picture has Brian holding his arms out as if he'd just exclaimed something really important. I tried to put on my best *Well, I am pretty good,* look. Elouise was smiling like she'd had botox put in, as she had been since she'd arrived even when Brian told her all about the turd in the fridge. The rest of the loyal workforce were either sneering or looked stony-faced, except Jeff that is. He was just staring up at the ceiling. God knows why. I never know with him.

I'll say this about the camera; it was cheap enough for me to buy it for office use and looks the business so that no one knew I skimped on the cost. The pictures that came out were OK, too. All I can say is, thank God it's a digital camera and I can doctor the photo to make everyone look like they're enjoying themselves. The miserable swine, anyone would think they didn't get a new kitchen to eat in. Maybe they were missing Donald and John.

Well, onwards and upwards. There's bath plugs need making and I'm the man to do the job. Well, to order other people to do the job, anyway.

-Mr Hogsbottom

DESIGNER INSPIRED LADIES HOLDALL (#HX3376) HANDBAG STYLISH TRENDY BAG IN BROWN

Looks great.

After my liability pay out I decided I would splash out on myself a little. I've always wanted a designer bag. This one looks just like the one I brought from the Chinese man on the market. However, this one has lasted more than three hours without falling apart.

I might have had to wear a neck brace for a few months and sit on a strange chair for my posture for the last few years of my employment, but It was certainly worth putting in a claim for. I've put the rest of the money in the bank and will spend it in my retirement.

Now I'm coming to the end of my employment, I'm going to start stealing office supplies. I plan to stockpile them and then open a little eBay shop when I'm retired. This bag has already helped me get a ream of paper out every other day this week. The straps have held up well, as has the zip.

-Margaret

HOW TO GET A JOB IN TOUGH TIMES
[KINDLE EDITION]

Works a charm.

Having recently got married, I thought it was high time I got a job. Well, my wife did, anyway. I agreed, too. We *did* need to spend less time together. Me being in and around the house all day was starting to annoy her.

Getting this book was her idea and a very good idea it was too. There's all sorts of bits and bobs inside that in all my years of attending the Job Centre I had never been told. I never knew it might be a good idea to ask friends and family if they knew of any jobs. I also never knew that when you went for a job, you needed to wear your wedding suit, but Janet, my wife, said that's what was suggested. So once my cousin, Jeff, had sorted me an interview at his place, I did. I also took on board the notes about not talking too much or sharing things that I may find funny but the employer wouldn't. It worked a treat. I just sat there and agreed that I could clean and move things from one place to another, didn't mention my pet chickens, and BAM! I was offered the job. It was a celebration in the Lamb and Whistle that night, I tell you. Me and Janet also celebrated when we got home. **big wink**

It's nice to get out the house. Sometimes it just feels bad there, like the evil chicken that attacked me is coming back to have another go. The extra money will come in handy, too. Auntie Julie says that she'll let me use her holiday home in

Hemsby once I can pay my way. Maybe it will be the time Janet and I and make some babies. We've had enough practise trying now.

-Brian

UPDATE

I've re-read the book since having started the job and there's some suggestions about how to integrate yourself into a new team. It did suggest not using humour to start with. However, I'm a funny guy, so I ignored that bit. I shouldn't have. Margaret was most upset that her handbag had been chucked on the roof. I really can't remember it being that bad of a thing to do at school. Clearly work is different to school, though. Margaret was screaming and shouting.

Jeff got the blame for doing it. Seeing how angry she was I did the decent thing and let him take the full blame for everything. I stood looking on from a handy gap between the vending machines where I'd wedged myself to watch the action. It's not like me and Jeff even look the same, so how she thought it was him she'd seen throwing it, I don't know. It was a great throw, though. Straight up and over the side of the guttering. If it hadn't been for the banging on the window from an angry Margaret I'd have done a little celebration dance.

The long and short of it is, listen to what this book says about using humour to gain friends. Jeff was my friend, anyway, so I didn't even gain him. Fair play to him though, he didn't grass me up.

If you want to get on in your job and do well in the interview to get it, this book is the one for you.

-Brian

ABOUT THE AUTHOR

Pete is 33 and lives with his wife, Lucie; daughter, Lilly; and their pet sofa, Jeff. He's been writing for just under three years and they've been pretty eventful; well, more eventful than he thought sitting on Jeff, typing, would be, anyway.

First published in the *Radgepacket* anthology with a story he'd written during month five of his new hobby, Pete's now featured in a total of ten different anthologies and has been amongst some very fine company. (Although he was the best in all of them, he knows that because both his mum and Jeff told him and they're both honest-to-God Christians ... possibly.)

Author of comedy e-books *The Village Idiot Reviews*, *The Office Idiot Reviews*, *The Idiot Government Reviews* and *More Village Idiot Reviews*, Pete has seen these books sell more than he ever thought they would, and he's hooked. *Dating in the Dark* is Pete's first self-published novel. His traditionally published novel, *So Low, So High*, was published by Caffeine Nights in June 2013.

Contact Pete:

Facebook:
https://www.facebook.com/pages/Pete-Sortwell/255907757862913

Twitter: @petesortwell

email: petesortwell@googlemail.com

OTHER TITLES

SO LOW, SO HIGH

Most people generally don't drink white cider for breakfast, don't use the aisle of Tesco as a toilet and don't steal from their family and friends. Simon Brewster does though. He's a doomed man. Living life day to day, stealing Edam balls and legs of lamb, ducking and diving his way from petty theft to dealer and back again. If he doesn't change his ways, he'll never see middle age, let alone old age.

He's seen his parents on their knees, crying, begging him to stop; he's been arrested by his former best mate; he's been hospitalised, all as a result of drugs and alcohol. It's just not enough to make him stop.

Simon lies to everyone, including himself. The truth is, he has no more idea why he does the things he does than you do. What he needs is a way out. But if such a thing exists, Simon hasn't had much luck finding it. He's powerless and his life is unmanageable to the point of insanity.

This is the story of Simon Brewster's last year using class A drugs. Join him as he crashes his way through police cells, courtrooms and display cabinets. One way or another, Simon will stop using drugs. But can the people that love him help him overcome his addictions before his addictions destroy him?

Available from Caffeine Nights Publishing.

THE VILLAGE IDIOT REVIEWS

Join Brian as he tries to woo the girl that works in the local shop; will passing out face down in super glue while trying to make her a gift hinder his chances of getting her to go out with him?

Will Father Frederick, an alcoholic vicar who has a slight issue with stalking, be able to win back the heart of a woman he loved a long time ago?

And will Ethel, who thinks that throwing hard rice instead of confetti in a bridegroom's face is an acceptable form of sport, be able to catch one of these two losers in love with her trick as they step out of the church on the happy day?

Written entirely in the form of product reviews, we guarantee you've never read a book quite like this before. Hilarious and wholly original, *The Village Idiot Reviews* pokes gentle fun at the more obscure corners of your favourite e-commerce sites – and introduces the most bonkers set of countryside dwellers since The Vicar of Dibley.

THE IDIOT GOVERNMENT REVIEWS

We've all seen the news over the last few years, watching in wonder and disbelief at the situations the people entrusted to run the country get themselves into and then proceed to lie their way out of. Just imagine, and this won't be hard, that they were so stupid that they wrote reviews of the items that got them into or out of their latest bit of trouble and posted them online.

Ted Williebond is angry, not only at having to settle for running the opposition, but also for the bullying he had to endure at school by Cameron Davies and Gary Osburn, who now run the Government and don't mind pointing that out to Ted every time they see him. Join Ted as he foolishly leaves reviews of such items as Silly String, vodka and thick curtains as he tries his hardest to bring down the coalition.

On the other side of the fence we've got Daniel Dangly, a foolhardy old school politician from Southamptonshire who, try as he might, cannot outrun the press, who seem to stalk him for easy stories; and Elouise Munch, a career girl more concerned about who's defaced her designer handbag than the people in her constituency.

Running the show though isn't Cameron Davies or Ted Williebond; in fact it is Betty Rivers, the CEO of Information Inc.

It can't work out well, can it?

Welcome to *The Idiot Government Reviews*.

THE COMPLETE IDIOT REVIEWS

The first three 'Idiot' reviews books are now available from Amazon in e-book format as a handy box set.

MORE VILLAGE IDIOT REVIEWS

It's been a year since their last outing. Brian, Ethel and Father Frederick are back with more village idiocy.

Frederick has injured his nipples in a vicious moped accident whilst on his honeymoon and no longer feels like a man. He's taken up the drink again and is making people's lives a misery with his antics again. He can't work out why strange men keep following him while he's out drink-driving, though.

Brian's concentrating on getting through married life while trying to find a hobby that doesn't hurt. His cousin Jeff (from *The Office Idiot Reviews*) has moved in for the summer and is on hand to help Brian with his assertiveness when he is bullied by the local biker, Jock.

Ethel has discovered that it was Denny who made her shopping trolley explode last year and with Denny now an adult and living outside the safety of the children's home, it won't be long before she exacts the revenge she's been after.

Meanwhile a battle for power is taking place at the manor house. Lord Monty, who ordered his title from the Internet, is in a battle of wills with his gamekeeper, Chopper. It's a never ending struggle which, time after time, leaves Monty either out of pocket, in pain or soaking wet.

Written entirely in the form of product reviews, we guarantee you've never read a book quite like this before. (Unless you read the first one.) Hilarious and wholly original, *More Village Idiot Reviews* introduces the most bonkers set of countryside dwellers you've ever had the pleasure of meeting.

DATING IN THE DARK
Sometimes Love Just Pretends To Be Blind

Jason is single and has been for all of his 32 years. It's depressing. But not as depressing as being told by his mother that he looks like Humpty Dumpty — after the accident. With a face that not even his own mother can love, it's hardly surprising that he'll try anything to get a woman to go out with him, even if it's only for a single date. With little interest in anything other than his quest for a woman and a nice bit of cod and chips, Jason needs to think outside the box if he's going to find someone who'll give him a chance. Along with Barry — his best mate — Jason comes up with the only thing he thinks will work: dating a blind woman. However, to do that, he needs to pretend he's blind himself, which is a lot harder than you might think ... especially when guide dogs are so hard to come by. Eventually Jason's efforts pay off and he meets Emma, a pretty professional with a host of friends. When he takes her out, they instantly hit it off. But will Jason be able to fool both Emma and her best friend Jerry into thinking he's blind? With everything to play for, Jason faces the biggest challenge of his life, and nobody — especially not him — can see how it'll all turn out.

Printed in Great Britain
by Amazon.co.uk, Ltd.,
Marston Gate.